# ALASKAN EAGLES

## STEVE SPEIGHTS

I see bald eagles everyday when I am out driving or in town where I live. It doesn't matter rain or shine, summer or winter they are there. My wife and I live in the Southeast part of Alaska, in a place nick named "The First City". We live in Ketchikan. If you took an Alaskan cruise in the past maybe you've stopped here. It's a great place to live especially if you enjoy nature.

I do not know the eagle population here, but we do have many full-time residents. Many juveniles are raised here as well every year. There are times when there are more eagles here, like when the salmon are here.

Watching eagles never gets old. Whether they are in flight or sunning themselves or drying out after a heavy rain, they are a beautiful and majestic bird to observe.

I am a local photographer and these are some of the eagles I have had the privilege of observing over the last few years.

Eagles enjoy high places to perch and rest.

Sometimes they just want to fly …

Though youths grow weary and tired, and vigorous young men stumble badly, yet those who wait upon the LORD will gain new strength; they will mount up with wings like eagles, they will run and not get tired, they will walk and not become weary.

Isaiah 40:30-31 NASB

Two birds in the air are better than one bird in the hand, especially if that one is an eagle...

Proverb of Steve

The Bald Eagle has been the national symbol of the United States of America since 1782

Rain or shine,

Summer or Winter,

Eagles can be seen.

A lone eagle looking for dinner.

*Eagles mate for life*

On the average it takes about 3 years for bald eagles to get their white.

Eagles can often be seen in groups while fishing or just catching some sun.

Eagles add to their nest's every year.

The average nest size is 4 to 5 feet in diameter and 2 to 4 feet in depth.

Hope you can see why I enjoy taking pictures and observing eagles. They truly are worthy of being our national bird, here in the U.S. of A.

Hope you have enjoyed them also. On my blog I have a short video that you can watch at:

www.sp8sstudio.com/2018/05/01/bald-eagles/

Steve Speights (pronounced Sp8S) is a photographer and lives in Ketchikan Alaska with his wife. He enjoys observing nature and being out in it. They also travel the states and he also has many travel photographs. Cruise ships and tourist activities are also something that he takes pictures of. He uses a Sony A77ii camera, as well as a DJI Phantom 4 drone. He is a certified drone pilot.

# Sp8s Studio

Thank you

www.sp8s-studio@outlook.com